MW01264848

Poems and Prayers for the Ups and Downs of Life

Poems and Prayers for the Ups and Downs of Life

Marsha Cain

To order additional copies of this book, contact:
Xlibris
844-714-8691
www.Xlibris.com
Orders@Xlibris.com
804546

Contents

POEMS AND PRAYERS FOR THE
TROUBLED HEART

POEMS AND PRAYERS FOR THE
SORROWING HEART

POEMS AND PRAYERS FOR
THE GRATEFUL HEART

Dedication

This book is dedicated to my parents, LaVerne and Roy Denial who instilled in our family a love of books and writing. Although they are both gone, they left behind special notes, poems, and letters which I continue to treasure.

My father Roy Denial was a professional writer most of his life. He wrote numerous articles that were featured in newspapers, magazines, and other publications, while also completing two novels during his retirement.

As a tribute to my father, I have taken the liberty of co-writing a poem with him, called "Hugs". In dedicating this book of poetry to my parents, I am thankful for all the hugs I have received and hope to pass some on to you!

Prologue

My interest in writing poetry began as a young child when I received a special birthday gift at age six – a copy of "A Child's Garden of Verses" by Robert Louis Stevenson.

This book opened my eyes to a world of play and imagination where the reader would delight in simple pleasures and pastimes.

As a child and teenager, I frequently found myself writing poems and songs to entertain myself and others. Over time, journalling became a standard practice that helped me to process my thoughts, express my feelings and cope with challenging situations.

So this book is the culmination of many years of processing, praying, and navigating through the "Ups and Downs of Life". I hope that my readers will find these poems helpful as they take their own journeys through uncharted waters.

Acknowledgements

One never accomplishes a goal without the encouragement of others. This is certainly true in my completion of this book. Over the years, I have been challenged to assemble my poems in a book for publication. I am thankful to the many relatives, friends and co-workers who have cheered me along the way.

However, I am most grateful to my husband Don for loving me and being willing to listen to my poems as I written and rewritten them. Our daughters Laura, Emily, and Liz provided me with many delightful memories, along with our son-in-laws and our fun-loving grandchildren. I am particularly indebted to my daughter Liz and her husband Sam Campbell in the preparation of my manuscript.

Finally, I want to acknowledge my brother Eric Denial and his wife Jane for all their love and support and for the faithfulness, they have shown through the "ups and downs" of life.

Love to All
Marsha

Poems and Prayers for the Young at Heart

Poetry for All

Poems for the mighty
Poems for the meek
Poems for the practical
And those still asleep

Poems for the promising
And poems for the poor
Poems for the folks we'd like
To send out the door
Poems for the experts
And poems for the mobs
And poems for the people
Who just lost their jobs

Poems for the weary
And poems for the wild
Poems for the grandmother
And poems for the child

Poems for the fidgety
And poems for the fair

Poems for all People
Everywhere
Poems for all People
Everywhere!

Write

Write, delete, write
Write, delete, write

Write something powerful
Write something great
Write something worthy
Something first rate

Write something crazy
Write something weird
Write something practical
Something to be feared

Write something witty
Write something grand
Something so prophetic
That the world will understand

Poetic License

Should I get a license?
Should I pay a fee?
To write my thoughts and memoirs
For someone else to see?

Word Power

Putting words together
In a syncopated style
Can get your heart a 'pumpin
For just a little while

Putting words together
Can create a song
One that has great meaning
Or one that lasts too long!

Putting words together
Can help you craft a tale
One that keeps you laughing
Or might land you in jail!

Moments

"A- ha" and "uh-oh"
Are words we often say
When good times and problems
Start to come our way

The "ah-ha moments"
Can give our hearts a song
But the "uh-oh moments"
Make us wonder
What went wrong

Balancing the "a-has"
With the "uh-ohs" is part
Of life's surprise

It surely keeps us guessing
Until the day we die!

Hugs

It's wondrous what a hug can do
A hug can say "I love you too"
Or maybe "Welcome back again"
"So great to see ya. Where you been?"

A hug can soothe a small child's pain
Or bring a rainbow after rain
A hug delights-It warms and charms
Maybe that's why God made arms

Hugs are great for dads and mothers
Sweet for sisters, swell for brothers
Chances are your favorite aunts
Love hugs more than their potted plants!

Old folks crave them; puppies love them
Even saints are not above them

A hug can help a broken heart
Or give a day a brand-new start
So, if you're wondering what to do
Just give someone a hug or two!

A Mother's Kiss

A mother's kiss
Tickles the belly
Wipes off the jelly

A mother's kiss
Lasts for a moment
But endures for a lifetime

The Dance

Girls arrive in fancy dress
Boys come too, with new pants pressed

Laughing girls with eyes aglow
Try to spot their favorite beau

Boys are cautious
Yet make their moves
Music plays, no time to lose

Will he ask her for a dance?
Is there time for some romance?

Nervous laughter plays its song
Time to dance and sing along

Girls share secrets
Boys share smiles
They're only children for a while

Guys and Gals

Guys like to fix things
Gals love to dream

Girls love to socialize
Boys like to scheme

Gals love to decorate
Guys like their space

Wonder what God was thinking
When He made the Human Race!

Moods

Some days we start out "in the groove"
But things happen, to change our mood

Sometimes our feelings
Grow and change
Sometimes we want them rearranged

Sometimes our feelings come and go
And where they go, we'll never know!

Spring's Song

Spring captures hearts when life seems new
It sings a song of flowers and dew

It sings a song of birds and trees
Oh, here it comes; I'm gonna sneeze!

Mother's Day Mania

Mother's Day is Coming
I have to get some gifts

For sisters, cousins, daughters
I think you get my drift

I have to plan a dinner
I have to clean my house

I have to buy a new dress
And make sure I kill the mouse

I have to get some cards
And drive out to the lake…

But since it's almost Mother's Day
I think I'll take a break!

Summer Days

Finding shade on summer days
Sipping fresh iced lemonade

Listening to the gentle grass
Hearing children as they pass

Seeing people, one by one
Doing chores as day is done

Birds still sing and children play
What a way to spend a day!

July 4th

Birthday candles fill the night
As red, white and blue take their flight
Soaring over crowds below
Fathers, mothers with child in tow

Smiling neighbors, merchants, friends
Sing our anthem once again
Asking God to show His grace
Renew our land and save this place!

Fair Time

Whirling rides
Spinning round
Don't you hear that happy sound?

Pizza, popcorn
Pop and such
It's fair food we love so much

Horses, rabbits
Sheep and goats
We love to touch their shiny coats

Cakes and pies and jellies too
Have you seen the ribbons
Red and blue?

Potatoes, onions, pumpkins, grand
The treasures of a farmer's hand

Games and prizes
Lights and smiles
A carnies' wish
A hopeful child

Music moves us
To the beat
We have to find a front row seat!

Friends and families
Neighbors, all
What a way to start the fall!

Demolition Derby

Tattered cars, muscle cars
Roaring in the mud
Old trucks, pickups
Hitting with a thud

Rednecks, a tattoo
Give yourself a break
Bluegrass, crabgrass
An excuse to stay up late

Hot dogs, popcorn
Give yourself a cheer
Good times, fun times
No time to show your fear

Late nights, date nights
Cheer with all your friends
Demolition derby
Let the good times begin!

A Redneck

What makes a guy a redneck?
Is it tattered jeans?
Is it a half-grown beard or
Country music dreams?

How 'bout worn-out cowboy boots
Or a southern drawl?
Maybe it's hard work
Or fighting in a brawl

Maybe he's a good ole boy
Just fishing by the creek
Or just another guy with snuff
Stuffed in his cheek

However you tag a country guy
With passion in his soul
You know it'll keep him going
'Til he's plum grown old!

Fishing

Fishing is an ancient art
Born in the soul
It found it's start
To think that you could find a fish
That just might make a yummy dish

Fishing's born of soul and faith
Knowledge, luck and lots of bait
Fishing is a quiet toil
With observation as its soil

Fishing gives a gentle man
Hope to believe that he really can
Catch the best fish of the day
And hope it doesn't get away!

The Man

He putters, he ponders
He what ifs, he wonders
He muses, confuses
And sometimes refuses

He cries out
He speaks out
He can rally a crowd
He's waiting, he's aching
He sometimes feels proud

He loves and he listens
At times his eyes glisten
He hopes and he schemes
As he copes and he dreams

So, join us in laughter
And happy ever after
As we cheer on this man
And all of his dreams

The Old Guys

The old guys at the restaurant
Love to swap tall tales
Of fighting wars or catching fish or
Just staying out of jail

They reminisce about their exploits
Their best friends or better days
They argue about politics and about the latest craze

They talk about Old Glory and what it meant to serve
They share pictures of those grandkids and
How some folks "got the nerve"

The guys like to tease their buddies or tell a corny joke
Or share a plate of pancakes or just drink a simple coke

They each promote their favorite team
or argue 'bout the stats
They trade the latest health news and
admit they're growing fat
They complain about the weather, their doctor, or their wife
They compare notes on how to fix a car, a faucet or a life

So, remember when you're stopping by
That restaurant just to eat
Give a wave to all the old guys
Who have made our lives a treat!

Home Renovation

Demo walls, rip out floors
Scrape wallpaper
And sand old doors

Pull out nails, re-glue wood
Sure hope this project's lookin' good

Touch up molding, secure the edge
Grab that hammer and that sledge

Trim off excess, say a prayer
Hope somehow, the end is near!

The Moving Dance

Sorting, packing
Fill a box
Taping, stacking
Where's my socks?

Reaching, stretching
Find that strap
Marking, stamping
Now take a nap!

When Days are Not Sunny

When days are not sunny and friends are not funny
And life is just boring and your husband is snoring
It's time for a new day, a get in the groove day

A let's get away day, and make time to play day
A why did we wait day, let's go for a date day

So cancel your work day, and make time to flirt day
It's a buy a new shirt day, no time to dig dirt day.

It's time for a start day, and not fall apart day
A feel like you're smart day, and time to make hay

Though it's not your birthday, it might be your worth day
When something you want, just might come your way

So, if life just seems boring and your husband is snoring
Put your feet on the flooring, turn your heart to adoring

Make plans for a bright day, a do it all-right day
A can't wait 'til it's night day,
Just take me away!

Dinner Dilemmas

What's up for dinner?
What should we all make?

How 'bout roast beef
Mashed potatoes or cake?

Or how 'bout corned beef
With cabbage and stew?

Or a roasted turkey?
Can I make it for you?

Or maybe you'd rather
Have chicken divan

Or Mexican fare or
Some food from Japan?

I could fix you waffles
With some bacon galore

Or cheesecake or pizza
I can find at the store

This is taking forever
To find your best food delight

I just feel exhausted
Think I 'll call it a night!

Pity Party

Let's have a "Pity Party!"
Sure hope that you can come
Bring tales of all your miseries
And when you're feeling glum

Bring along a boring friend
And bad news from near and far
Oh, remember that this party is
Come, just as you are!

Couplet

Mumble and Grumble and Gossip and Glee
Can destroy a friendship in one-two-three!

Someone's Turning 60

Someone's Turning 60
Oh, who could that be?
Someone's getting older within our family tree

Someone's turning 60
Now how can that be true?
That someone turning 60
Just might be me and you!

Baby Boomers

Oh, we're the Baby Boomers
We were destined to be young
We grew up on the Beatles
On free love, and having fun

As youth we loved our freedom
And we sometimes spoke our mind
But the years have gone so quickly
We've just lost track of time

We're a special generation
And lots of changes we have seen
From hula hoops to hippies
We've shared in many a dream

A peaceful world we've wanted
And still, we hope to see
A better, greener planet
Where there's hope for you and me

So, as we face life, aging
With new days, still in store

We'll keep alive our freedom
And always look for more

Though we are Baby Boomers
With gray hairs upon our head
We're not slated for our rockers
Or crawling back in bed

Oh, we'll keep our dreams a 'goin
No matter what's in store
'Cause we've always caused commotion
And we've always wanted more

Crazy Things

What crazy things did you do before you turned 22?
What fun things could be in store if you lived to be 94?

When I was young, I thought I'd be….
A millionaire by 33

When I was young, I thought I'd find
A brand-new way to just save time

If I could be like other folks
I might learn to laugh at other's jokes

I'd try to learn to read more books
And give more attention to my looks

I think I'd try to travel more
And spend some time along the shore

I'd try to listen a with my heart
And give my heart a brand-new start

I'd try to learn from day to day
And not let my troubles get in my way

Remembering

How do we remember a million things each day?
Like what's her name? Where's my phone?
And where'd I put my cane?

Some say we make connections
With the different things we know
But lately my connections
Are acting kind of slow

Perhaps I need a tune-up
To put my mind in gear
Or just a cup of coffee
Or a nice cold can of cheer!

New Glasses

I got myself new glasses
And hoped they'd help me see
Smiles on children's faces
A new show on TV

I hoped I'd read much better
And could keep up with my chores
But I can't find my glasses
So, I'll have to look some more!

My Feet

Oh feet, oh feet
Take care of me
Hold me up and walk for me

Let me move from heel to toe
Keep me upright, though I may be slow

Feet, oh feet
Let's just be friends
Keep me standing once again

I will wash and care for you
Keep me upright
'til this day is through!

My Mind

In my mind, there's words to say
But sometimes, my thoughts get in the way
I wish my brain would try to work
So, I won't feel like a jerk!
Dear Jesus, save me from this day!

Upstairs

I need to go upstairs and rest my weary head
I need to go upstairs and find my way to bed
I need to go upstairs for day has turned to night
I need to go upstairs, but I hate to make the flight!

A Colonoscopy

A colonoscopy
A colonoscopy
Time for you to get your colonoscopy

You get some sympathy
You get some sympathy
You get some sympathy
With your colonoscopy

You get a nap for free
You get a nap for free
You get a nap for free
With your colonoscopy

You might save your family tree
Might save your family tree
You might save your family tree
With a colonoscopy!

The Christmas Mess

My Christmas memory's fading. I can't find all my cards
My Christmas list has blown away.
It's somewhere in my yard

My tree is tipping slightly. Old Santa lost his cap
And my dear, sweet husband, just wants to take a nap!

Oh, the Christmas mess, the Christmas mess
When will it all get done?
Why do all those Christmas shows
Show people having fun?

My cookies are all burning, I forgot to cash my check
Why are there wrappings and the ribbon 'round my neck?

Is there a gift for Mary? Is there a card for Paul?
Have you seen all that traffic on your way down to the mall?

Oh, the Christmas mess, the Christmas mess
When will it all get done?
Why do all those Christmas shows
Show people having fun?

I've lost the names of all my children, perhaps I have a son
I have to get these gifts all mailed, before December 31!

Is there candy for the stockings and toys for all the kids?
Sometimes I get excited and think I'll flip my lid!

Oh, the Christmas mess, the Christmas mess,
When will it all get done?
Why do all those Christmas shows
Show people having fun?

Going to the Emergency

Oh, I have been away you see
Going to the Emergency

Nurses, aides and doctors, too
Sticking, poking; it's what they do

IVs, vitals. What's your weight?
Do you drink or stay up late?

When did you last take your pill?
In the ER, I know the drill

Where's your pain? Does this hurt?
Are you tired or out of work?

Do you have an allergy?
Were you asleep at half past three?
Here's a bed pan, and a snack
In a minute, "we'll be back!"

Yes, I have been away you see
Going to the emergency!

Taking Care

Well, I don't need
A password, a photo, or ID
God is always listening
And He's taking care me

I'm so glad that He's my Savior
And He has set me free
Thank you, dear Jesus
For taking care of me

God's "line" is never busy
When we call upon His Name
Our pleas don't go unnoticed
What a wonderful refrain

I have a God who loves me
And He's always "checking in"
I'm so very glad
That I can always count on Him

I'm never put on "busy"
"On call back" or "on hold"

God's so understanding
So, I can just be bold

I can come before my Savior
And can always "make my plea"
So glad the Lord is taking
Special care of me

Thank you, Lord, for taking
Such special care of me!

The Obits

I must be getting older, reading the Obits
Wondering about old friends
And just where on earth they sit

Wondering, just wondering
If they ever think of me
Perhaps they're reading the Obits
Just looking there for me!

So What

So what if you have a new grey hair upon your head
Just be thankful you're alive
And not wishing you were dead!

Decades

Turning Ten is a treasured time
Of baseball games and counting dimes

Turning Twenty is a time to dance
And maybe find some sweet romance

Turning Thirty can be a race
With no wrinkles yet upon your face

Forty can find us on the move
With much to do but much to lose

Turning Fifty may cause alarm
We feel we're losing all our charms

Turning Sixty may seem great
If retirement is your fate

Seventy may find us with new goals
Though we may feel we're growing old

Eighty years may come so fast
We wonder how long our life may last

When celebrating Ninety years
We know we've conquered many fears

Now turning One Hundred
Now that sounds old

But oh, the stories that can be told!

Funny Lines

Funny lines and funny poems
Put my heart at ease

Spicy sauce and pepper spice
Makes me want to sneeze

Hiccup coughs and blessed burps
All want to have their say

Oh, what funny music
For such a funny day!

Betty Spaghetti

Betty Spaghetti is the fastest girl in town
She can make her bed and clean her room
While you're still lying down

She can brush her hair and floss her teeth
While you're thinking of a song

She can climb real high and crawl real low
And she dances with the dawn

She has lots of great adventures
That she'd love to share with you

So, get ready for Miss Spaghetti
She'll have lots of fun with you!

The Broom

There once was a broom that was lazy
It just sat around acting crazy
It never would work and just like a jerk
Made messes that made the air hazy

The Jolly Woman

There once was a woman so jolly
She never could be melancholy
She would laugh and smile and after a while
The whole town forgot all their follies!

The Computer

There was a computer so loaded
It felt rather tired and bloated
When a man pressed "delete"
It felt rather sweet
So the computer
Just emptied and floated!

Fancy Girl

Making faces is so much fun
When smiling in the blazing sun

Crinkled noses, rosy cheeks
Darling hats and hair so sleek

Fancy bracelets, painted toes
Sharing giggles and dress-up clothes

Pearly necklace and diamond rings
Twirly dresses and shiny things

Lovely laces, hair in curls
These are the dreams
Of a fancy girl!

Great Day

Knock, knock who's there?
Let's make another joke

Let's tell another story
About some silly, funny folk

Let's draw another picture
Let's read another book

Let's play a special game
And let's learn how to cook

Let's fly another kite
Let's sing a brand-new song

Let's tell another story and
This day just can't go wrong!

Silly Boy

Tickle a pickle
And break a leg

Sniff a whiff
And fry a cake

Puff a pancake
And jump for joy

These are the games
Of a silly boy!

Baby Rock

We're gonna rock our little baby
Every single day
Hula Boola

We're gonna rock our little baby
Every single day
Hula Boola

We're gonna rock our little baby
Every single day

'Cause our baby loves to Rock and Roll
Rock and Roll
Yeah!

My Room

My room's a disaster
My clothes I can't find
My homework is missing
I've just found some slime!

Some toys I've found broken
Some dirt's on the floor
I've found an old picture
Of what, I'm not sure!

My mom will be angry
My gramma will too
If I have to tell them
A frog's in my shoe!

My lunchbox is missing
Some food's lost its way
The trash should be emptied
Sometime later today

I think I'll keep playing
But, maybe instead
I should clean up my room
And look under my bed!

Grandma Says

My Grandma says
"Life is a race"
And it's time that
I picked up my pace

To go to bed
To go to school
I have to learn the Racing Rules

Is it fast or is it slow?
And just how far do I need to go?

I need to know just what to do
So, I can see when my race is through

Grandma says when
My race is done that
I could be having lots of fun

There are lots of races, though
Some might be fast and others slow
Most are at an easy pace
But sometimes I have to really race

There's a lot of racing in my day
Before I can go out and play
Some days I have to race to school
To a friend's or to the pool

On other days I have to race to eat
To clean my room and make it neat
Sometimes we race to the car
To go to church or a bazaar

Sometimes we race to the store
To the doctor and so much more
I'm learning now to run my race
To get things done at a certain pace

Because I'm following the Racing Rules
Life's much more fun
And I'm on time for school!

Math Magic

Oh, to be able to count fast, by ten
Divide by five, and multiply again

To measure inches, in feet, and yards
And just remember those old flash cards

To know when to "take away" and when
I need my numbers to stay

To know when ratios have their place and when
Decimals might just need their space

To know how to find "x" and "y"
And better yet, not start to cry

Oh, it would be so very grand
If I could only understand
Why I need to know of PI
When math class comes rolling by

Or how 'bout when it's time for me
To know the age of a tree or

Measure horses by hands or feet
Or learn if a number, I should delete

I think I could be very smart
If I knew all my facts by heart
Maybe if I knew these things
I could be as rich as kings

I could understand the national debt
And then live, somehow, without regret
Then it might be, so plain to me
To know that math is the key!

Who and What and Where and When

Who and What and Where and When
Loved to play again and again

They loved to dance
They loved to sing
They loved to do most anything

They loved to jump
They loved to run
They always had the best of fun

Sometimes they'd go on weekend trips
To the oceans on new cruise ships
At other times they liked to fly
Or catch a bus that was rolling by

Who and What and Where and When
Had many interests and many friends

But their greatest treat of all
Came when the leaves began to fall

For they would make a special stop
At the school just down the block

And help children learn to write
Creating stories true and bright!

Winter, Winter

Winter, winter
What's your tale?
That speaks to us, through wind and gale

That speaks to us
In soft, wet snow
That speaks to us, wherever we go

Lines

Timelines
Waiting lines
Grocery lines
School lines
Deadlines
Traffic lines
Fine lines
Lifelines
Funeral lines
So many lines in life

Poems and Prayers for the Troubled Heart

In the Day of Trouble

In the day of trouble
When fear is in the air
And worry finds us weeping
With our souls tied to a chair

We worry, fret and grumble
As we hope for grace and peace
But it's only through our Savior
That our souls find sweet release

When Fear Comes

When fear comes knocking at the door
And worry comes to bring you more

When sadness overtakes the room
and loneliness starts to loom

It's time to breathe
It's time to pray

Oh, Jesus take these thoughts away!

Twin Towers

The Twin Towers came down that day
As Americans took time to pray

Over twenty years have come and gone
Have we lost our nation's song?
Have we lost our soul, our way?
Is it too late for us to pray?

To our Father, Savior, Lord?
Can we be of one accord?
Seeking You above the rest
Help us Lord. We're in a mess!

September 11

They blew up our world today
With crashing planes gone astray

The towers fell in disarray
As frantic people cried and prayed

They blew up our world today
As hate and terror came our way

So many lost, yet some were saved
Can we forget this awful day?

They blew up our world today
It seems surreal. We need to pray

We need to know and understand
How this could happen in our land?

Did you Hear?

Lord, did you hear?
Did you see all the death and the debris?

Lord, did you notice?
Did you smell the raging fire that burnt like hell?

God, were you there in our grief, in our tears and disbelief?
Were you there when our hope died?
Were you there when we all cried?

It's 3 a.m.

It's 3 a.m.
I cannot sleep
A war is coming, the pain runs deep

Bombs and soldiers, tanks and crew
Are all deciding what to do

Leaders talk, yet war prevails
The newsman waits for breaking tales

As mothers cry and children sleep
The world's aflame
It's time to weep!

Their Son

Their son went off to war today
They asked in church for us to pray

Secret weapons, gas and oil
UN inspections, a wicked toil

The Middle East, Iraq, Iran
I really do not understand

My nephew's going off to war
Like many soldiers have done before

I never thought I'd see this day
I guess they're right, we need to pray

But pray for what?
For peace and love
For God's protection from above

For God to stretch out His Hand
And help us all to understand

Through the years of history
Peace and War
A mystery

Leaders come and leaders go
Our Peace, uncertain, this I know

How?

How do you explain a war?
To little children, only four

How do you explain the truth?
To old men and dying youth

How do you watch and pray?
As you begin a brand-new day

How do you understand?
When war seems so close at hand

The Veteran

The man was a soldier
Way back in his youth
He fought for his country
For freedom, for truth

He fought for his family
And for those not yet born
He fought for his soul
That seemed so forlorn

Now battles are ugly
And war- just like hell
And some of his secrets
He never will tell

So as he grows older
With much of life gone
He knows he was brave
And he knows he was strong

But sometimes at night
When there is quiet all around
He still hears the anguish
Of war's deadly sound

The Sounds

The Sounds of Fear scream
As the Voice of Hope beacons

The Sounds of Rage clamor
As the Voice of Love soothes

The Sounds of Silence deafen
As the Voice of Faith prevails

Wounds

Nurses nurse them
And sailors curse them
Open wounds for all to see

Nurses nurse them
And sailors curse them
Find some relief on bended knee

The Price

The price of freedom
The pain of war
The price of freedom
From years before

The price of freedom
What will we pay?
The price of freedom
Will it blow away?

Paducah

Paducah, Santee, Columbine
Another day, another crime

Another kid, another school
Why don't we teach the Golden Rule?

Pencils, paper, books and guns
Are the shootings ever done?

Students, teachers, parents, friends
When will the bloodshed ever end?

Peaceful Savior

Peaceful Savior
Loving Lord
How cruel the gun
How sharp the sword

Dear sweet Jesus
Loving Friend
When will the violence ever end?

Baby Jesus, born to die
Your first word was but a cry!

Though we suffer
Though we moan
We know that we are not alone!

Peaceful Savior
Loving Friend
You'll be with us to the end!

Slaughter of the Innocents

The Slaughter of the Innocents
In every age and clime

Has brought people to their knees
What horrific crimes!

Whether on the banks of Jordon
Or on Great Britain's shore

The Slaughter of the Innocents
Can be tolerated no more!

Mad World

Oh, Lord, the world is growing mad!
Bombings, killings
Oh, how sad

Unsuspecting children, teens
Cruelly losing youthful dreams

Parents searching, in dismay
For children lost on this day

Whether in the Middle East, Africa
Or modern Greece, Germany
France or ancient Rome
In a child's world
It's all called "home"

In Syria, Great Britain, too
In Tel Aviv, could this be a true?
In New York and Boston town
Terrorists want to take us down!

Lord, may our leaders, great and small
Do their best to save us all
May you give us wisdom, power
To aid us in this crucial hour!

Disturbed

He wasn't on YouTube, or Facebook, or Twitter
His personal effects, scattered in litter

A middle-aged man, with no hope in sight
Died of exposure on a cold, dreary night

No family to claim him
No friends far or near
They'll bury his body
Somewhere around here

What was he missing?
What have we lost?

A homeless encounter
How much was the cost?

Pushed to Prayer

You might not be a faithful soul
Prone to hymns that might make you whole

But as you go throughout your life
You might find yourself filled with strife

You might learn that it's hard to love
And feel thankful for gifts from above

You might find it's hard to forgive
And sometimes just hard to live

You might get mad when you hit your nail
Or fear you have to go to jail

You might get annoyed with some folks you meet
And say some things you should delete

You might feel sad when you're all alone
And when your best prayers are just a groan

These are the times you can be pushed to prayer
Wondering if God is really there

Wondering if you've lost your way and if
Now's your chance to learn to pray

These are the times to seek the Lord
And discover something from His Word

A time to pour out your soul
So, God has the chance to make you whole

A Single Mother

A single mother giving birth
Feels alone upon this earth

Giving life, yet filled with doubt
Learning what life is all about

Needing care, support and hope
Who's around to help her cope?

Hungry Children

Hungry children come to school
Not learning well the Golden Rule

Not learning how to hope, to share
How can they learn to read, to care?

Cry Out

Cry out
Cry out for the children
Cry out
Cry out for the children

Listen hard as their voices scream

Cry out while our souls are mourning
Cry out for our hearts are longing
For their precious voices to be heard

Cry out, cry out for our nation
Cry out as we seek restoration
Cry out as our nation screams

Cry out for some understanding
Cry out though the world's demanding
That our silenced voices not be heard

Cry out in the towns and cities
Cry out though it isn't pretty

Cry out
Cry out, my friend, cry out

Cry out, cry out to the Savior
Cry out as we seek God's favor
Cry out as our cities burn

Cry out, while our souls are mourning
Cry out, as our hearts are longing
For God's voice to still be heard

Cry out for some understanding
Cry out, though the world's demanding
That God's truth not be heard

Cry out in the towns and cities
Cry out though it isn't pretty

Cry out
Cry out my friend, cry out

Hurricane Harvey

Victims of the flood, the storm
Striving hard to keep their homes

Fighting hard, with all their might
Stalking fear into the night

The water's rising, covering grass
Raging rivers, flowing fast

Churning floods, a record storm
Lives chaotic, hearts are torn

Prayers are offered, help is sent
Neighbors clamor, time is spent

Rising rivers, swirling streams
Crushing waters, crushing dreams

Rooftop rescues, boats in sight
Look out, neighbor, "hold on tight!"

Waiting, praying, pressing on
Longing for a sun-filled dawn

Hoping with a wish, a prayer
That our lives will still be here!

Irma's Plea

Irma's pressed on every side
A hurricane, oh so wide

Moving fast near Floridian shores
Alarms, alert. Don't ignore!

Time to leave. Time to go
We're leaving everything we know!

Get our water, food and such
Coats and blankets, shoes and stuff

Find our flashlights, cash and cards
Grab your phones. I hope they're charged!

Put the kids in the car
We may be travelling very far!

Pictures, papers, treasures too
I sure hope we all make it through!

First aid kit and meds to take
The storm is coming
No time to waste!

Say a prayer, shed a tear
Lord, take away our fears!

Hope

When folks are feeling in despair
And disasters come from everywhere

A little hope from someone new
Might be the thing that pulls them through

It might be someone far away
Whom they've never met
But who starts to pray
Asking God for a better day

So, as you're looking all around
And wonder where some hope is found

Make sure you look inside your heart
And give someone a brand-new start

Bonded

Bonded by Hope
Bonded by Power
We are bonded by Love in this very hour

Bonded by Joy
Bonded by Grief
We are bonded by Love in this troubled hour

Bonds that we know
Bonds that we share
Are God's gifts to us, though, we are unaware

Prayers Like Raindrops

Prayers like raindrops
Cover the earth
Bring us life
Through sorrow and mirth
Bring us life
Though days be long
Bring us joy
When we need a song

"Flatten the Curve"

"Flatten the curve"
The phrase we've all heard

In every city, throughout the land
We're still trying to understand

We think of our families and all of our friends
And wonder when we will see them again

We think of our jobs, our money, our life
And wish that our world wasn't so filled with strife!

Social Distance

We must keep a social distance
So our body has resistance

To mitigate the spread
Of the corona virus dread

A Covid Prayer

We're hurting deep inside, Lord
Brought down by covid care

Bodies are so broken
And fear is everywhere

We're feeling overwhelmed, Lord
Too much sickness and disease

Please come and heal us Lord
And put our minds at ease

We're feeling isolated
From family far and near

We're wishing that our best friends
Would just suddenly appear

We're angry with the whole world
'Cause we can't seem to agree

We're yearning for your refuge
For some peace and unity

We're longing so for, Jesus
Who knew the suffering on a tree

We're needing your forgiveness
So we can be set free

We're desperate for a Savior
Who can make this world all right

We're pleading for our prayers
To be answered in the night

Our burdens are so heavy
And we don't know what to do

Please give us hope and guidance
So we can make it through

Truth, Truth

Where is the truth?
We thought we once knew you
Back in our youth

We thought we once knew you
Before lies set in
We thought we once knew you
When you were our friend

Data, Data Everywhere

Data, data
Everywhere
Recording every word

Data, data
Everywhere
Where can the truth
Be heard ?

Data, data everywhere
Recording all our life

Data, data everywhere
Causing fear and strife

Facebook Fears

Don't give all your news to Facebook
And share all your thoughts and dreams
Save those for a real friend
And not for Facebook schemes!

Faith and Fear

Faith and fear, a balancing act
Trying to weigh, hope with fact

Trying to keep trust alive
Knowing God is by our side

Why Do I Worry?

Why do I worry when things don't go right?
Why do I worry in the dead of the night?

Why am I worried and so filled with care?
When my Savior says
"I'll still be here"

Lord, Help Me

Lord, help me
When I'm angry and disappointed too
When life makes no sense, with all I'm going through

Lord, please forgive me
When I've failed you once again

When my pride or impatience has
hurt a loved one or a friend

Lord, change me
When my bitterness has hurt the ones that I love

Lord, please forgive me
And teach me how to love

My Heart

Lord, heal my heart for it is worn
Ripped apart, tattered, torn

Lord, guard my heart
And make it strong
That I might serve You all day long

Guard my heart and make it true
So I might be true to You

Brought to Tears

Lord I have seen many hurtful things
Things that have brought me to tears

Things that have frightened me
Things that have worried me
Things that have brought me to tears

Lord I have seen hurting souls in my day
Folks who have brought me to tears

Folks who have frightened me; even incited me
Folks who have brought me to tears

Lord, you have brought me through so many trials
And comforted me along the way

Lord, you have carried me
You have protected me
When life has brought me to tears

I want to praise you
I want to thank you
That you have given me life

You have sustained me
You have sheltered me
When life has brought me to tears

Listening

Listening is an art, they say
To help us focus throughout the day

To understand a point of view
To know what someone's going through

To understand another's plight
To separate what's wrong, what's right

To listen, care and understand
To offer hope, a helping hand

Forgiveness Speaks

Forgiveness calls in quiet ways
As we struggle through darkened days
As we moan and cry and wail
Or just review our awful tale

Forgiveness speaks in quiet tomes
As we walk through our lonely rooms
As we ponder our fears and doubts
Wondering what it's all about

Forgiveness speaks with hope and love
With new beginnings from above
Forgiveness speaks when life is sad
And only grace can make us glad

When only love can find a way
When forgiveness speaks
It's time to pray

Reconciliation

Angry words, hurting hearts
Divide our families into parts

Misunderstandings, unkind words
Put our minds into a blur

Pride and passions, spoken fears
Fill our lives with many tears

What's the answer to our fate?
Is forgiveness much too late?

Can we look at our loss?
And see Christ dying on a Cross?

Can we look with loving eyes?
To know our family is our prize?

Can we listen, love and look?
And get direction from the Book?

Can we turn a loving ear?
To learn the lessons, we could hear?

Can we place our burdens down?
And in Christ, with Him be found?

Our Help

God you are our Help in Trouble

You are our Strength each day
When we lose hope and falter
When we can't find our way

You are our Hope in suffering

When we feel weak and frail
You are our Refuge in the Storm
And with You, we will prevail

Only Your Love

Only your love Lord can span the oceans
Only your love Lord can calm the seas

Only your love Lord can make all the difference
In this troubled heart for me

Lord, You have made the mountains
Lord, You have made the seas

Your beauty reigns in creation
Please make all the difference in me

Only your love, Lord can heal the broken
Only your love, Lord can calm the seas

Only your love, Lord can make all the difference
In this troubled world for me

Lord, You have made the mountains
Yes, You have made the seas

Your beauty reigns in creation
Please make all the difference in me

An Evening Prayer

Lord, as we all lay down to rest
For some this day has been a test

A time of struggle, a time of woe
Not certain just where they should go

For some, this day has been a joy
The birthday of a girl or boy

For some, this day has been too long
With many problems and things gone wrong

For some folks, this day has been a blur
Way too busy, with life unsure

Some folks have had the best of days
With achievements great and marked with praise

Tonight, some need Your Special Touch
Because today was just too much

Lord, as you hear a dark world's prayers
May we find You in our prayers

My Troubles

I put my troubles in a box
And closed them up with dirty socks

I put my sorrows on a chair and hoped
I'd never find them there

I threw my hurts across a wall
But they bounced back and made me fall

So I locked my troubles in a room
But soon it became a tomb

So I hid my sorrows in a drawer
But they kept growing
And brought me more

Then I cut my heartaches up in sheets
And tried to stack them up real neat

I wore my sorrows on my face
But I became a great disgrace

I tried to sell my hurts away
But no one had enough to pay

So I put my troubles back to bed
But they kept screaming in my head

After all the heartaches I'd been through
I wondered what next, I should do

So I took my troubles to the Cross
I counted them and suffered loss

I found a Savior, bruised for me
Some said He died upon a tree

Some said He came to take my place
When full of sin, I met disgrace

I saw a Man, full of woe
Misunderstood and weeping so
A God-come down to ransom me
For all my hurt on Calvary

I saw a Man with loving eyes
With outstretched hands

He knew my lies
He knew my pain
Would I ever be the same?

So, I took my troubles to the Cross
I counted them and suffered loss

I found a Friend, forever true
Who understands and helps me too

He takes away my sin and shame
And helps me live. He took my blame

He carries me when I am weak
And covers me when I retreat

He is a refuge from my storms
When feeling bad and oh, forlorn

He can put my fears to rest
Hides my shame, yet knows me best

He can understand my moods
When I ache and when I brood

He alone can guide my way
When I can't see the light of day

When I can't make it on my own
I go to Him. He's on the throne

I'm glad I found a Friend, so true
Who picks me up when I am blue

Poems and Prayers for
the Sorrowing Heart

Late Night Call

A late night call
A call of dread
We hear the words
They're spoken, said

Yet our minds begin to fail
We cannot fathom the ugly tale
We try to listen. We try to think
But our mind is on the blink

We take a breath in disbelief
We're on a journey of love and grief

Family and Friends

Family and friends gathered near
Respects to pay
Their words to cheer

Their hugs to give, a touch, embrace
Oh, what comfort
To see their face

Family and friends gathered here
They helped us out
They kissed our tears

But now, they're gone
And we're still here, with all our questions,
Our aches, our fears.

Is this a dream?
Will it soon end?
And we will have you back again?

The Waves of Grief

Grief ebbs and flows
Like waves on the sea
Sometimes a storm
Sometimes a plea

Sometimes a memory
Sometimes a doubt
When will we learn
What life's all about?

Our Deepest Prayers

Our deepest prayers are groanings
That others may not hear
Though they stand beside us
And help us wipe each tear

Our deepest prayers are groanings
Like we have never known
As we seek God's comfort
When our loved one's been called Home

Our deepest prayers are groanings
That we don't quite understand
For we are only human
We are merely man

Tears

Tiny droplets

One
By
One

Cleanse
Our souls
When day is done

They mend our hearts
Restore our peace

And with God's help
We find release

Morning

I look around my awful bed
My life's a burden and a dread

Yet You still love me
I know not how
Please don't forsake me
Please, not now

Your light still glimmers
Your strength still shines
Help me remember
That You're still mine

Satan's still our ancient foe
Who tries to block Your heavenly glow

You're still the Victor, come what may
Dear Jesus, save me from this day!

Oh Lord, be with me in Your grace
And make me find my life's true place

I Want to Pray

I want to pray
I know not how
I close my eyes
On knees I bow

I cry, I weep
I pause, I groan
That's how I take it
To God's throne

But God somehow takes my fears
Unlocks my heart
And wipes my tears

He alone can show me grace
That makes my soul
A better place

"Lord, teach me how to pray
So, I might follow You today."

My Plea

Oh, Lord, give to me a song
My days are bleak. My nights are long

Lord, teach me again to sing
That I might worship the Heavenly King

Routine

Alarm goes off, another day,
Who said, "It's time to feel okay?"

Do they not know? Or understand?
I'm living still in Sorrow's Land.

Silence

Wanting silence to fill the air
When grief has filled the room
Hearing silence everywhere
Just like an empty tomb

No time for thoughts or questions
No time for keeping score
No newfound revelations
For someone knocking at the door

The silence grows and fills the heart
Weakened by life's storms
The heavy weight of silence
Of feeling so forlorn

Grief

Such a dark and lonely place
Filled with fear and disgrace

Shrouded in a cloak of dread
I find no rest upon my bed

The night calls through endless days
Uncertain of life's shining rays

The ticking clock invades the night
Bringing with it dread and fright

Oh, to release the gloom
From my mind's shattered tomb

A tiny light, a hope, a spark
Take me from this living dark

Take me from this awful place
Where I see the human race

Yet a glimmer, yet a ray
Touch me, make me new today

Laughter

Laughter's still our mighty friend
Our age-old joy, our hearts sure mend

Laughter's in God's precious plan
To heal our hearts from God to Man

To heal us of life's hurts and pain
To give us joy, while life remains

To laugh again, how can it be?

When life has taken you from me
When darkness is still all I see

Oh, help me laugh, and set me free!

Loss

When all seems lost, and faith is dim
It's our best time to still seek Him
To know His suffering, pain and loss
That led Him to a deadly cross

He bears our burdens one by one
For He is Jesus, God's own Son

Into the dark hole of despair
Our Savior crawls to find us there

Needy, wanting, fearful, sad
He sheds His light to make us glad

He understands our fearful ways
That have blackened darkened days

He knows our hurts, our grief, our pain
For He has scars that still remain

He gathers us with loving arms
To share with us his Godly charms

A fairer Friend, we could not find
One who loves us, and is kind

Unwelcome Guests

Sorrow moved in today
And tried to take my joy away

Fear and guilt took their place
Accusing me with much disgrace

Lord, remove these unwanted guests
And give my heart much needed rest

Perspective

Without Love, there is no Grief
Without Faith, only Disbelief

Without Trust, no Hope or Care
Without God, there's just Despair

But with God, there's Hope and Faith
True Forgiveness, Amazing Grace

With God, there's Love and Peace
Our Heart's True Comfort
Our Soul's Release

Longing

Longing for her husband's touch
The widow cries, "This is too much!"
Tossing in her lonely bed
She cries to God
No words are said

There alone with midnight dreams
She feels the tears, the inner scream
She shuts her eyes
She tries to pray
Her new life is in disarray

She feels the cold of winter's night
And thinks of how her love took flight
She smiles again with burning tears
Remembering their early years

She wonders how he loved her so
And just how God could let him go

The Widow

Who comforts the widow in the still of the night?
When family has scattered
And her memories take flight

Who comforts the widow when life seems a dream
And time, oh so fleeting
A wicked, cruel, scheme

With words from the Savior
And prayers of the saints
Mingled with life's many complaints

She calls out to heaven
With tears and with grief
Asking her Lord for some peace and relief

With Angels descending and prayers all around
The quiet Redeemer
Is sure to be found

The Love of the Father
And the care of a Dove
Quietly offering mercy and love

A Soldier's Lament

A soldier, a soldier
A rugged soldier
Fighting for life
And fighting for peace

A soldier, a soldier
A wounded soldier
Fighting for life
And fighting for peace

A soldier, a soldier
A treasured soldier
Dying for love
And dying for peace

Memories Linger

Memories linger
Our thoughts embrace
As we recall a younger face

A young child dancing in the sun
When days were new
And days were young

When days were happy
Young and free
Our love was bright
Like you and me

Though years have come and others gone
We still remember his precious song

Now with the angels, he must sing
For he is worshipping the King

Questions

You were a child of questions
Questions, great and small
Like why a bird stands to sleep
While others creep and crawl

You asked about the stars
That shine brightly in the sky
You filled our lives with questions
As the days went rolling by

We heard each of your questions
They were tender and so dear
Oh, how we loved our playtimes
And just to have you near

We loved our times for boating
And playing in the sun
We watched you throw a football
And loved to see you run

You loved to smile for pictures
With mom and dad and sis

You filled our lives with laughter
With snuggles and a kiss

And now that you have left us
For a better place
We're left asking questions
About the human race

For we know that you've been welcomed
By Jesus Christ, our Lord
Who holds eternal answers
From the Father and His Word

Someday we'll know all answers
Of how this came to be
And just how much God loves us
Will be plain for all to see

But now we seek God's comfort
His courage and His grace
And know they'll be some answers
When we see His Shining Face

Come, My Love

Oh come, my love and grieve with me
We've lost our son. How can this be?

I need your arms to comfort me
Come, be my love and grieve with me.

Oh come, my love and grieve with me
My soul seems lost. How can this be?

I need your love to comfort me
Come, be my love and grieve with me

Oh come, my love and grieve with me
My faith seems lost, how can this be?

I need your hands to pray for me
Come, be my love and grieve with me

Oh come, my love and grieve with me
My way seems lost, how can this be?

I need your arms to carry me
Come, be my love and grieve with me

Oh come, my love and grieve with me
My life seems lost, how can this be?

I need your love to set me free
Come, be my love and grieve with me

Plight

When God is silent
And I've lost my way
When confusion beckons
My soul away

When God seems distant
And I have no cause
It's time for me to sit and pause

It's time for me to hunger, thirst
For God's provision is not my curse

Will I trust Him?
Come what may
Even though I've lost my way

Even though I've shed some tears,
Has God failed me through all these years?

Or has He been a Friend so true,
Who still whispers, "I love you."
He offers me His gentle hand,
Listens, cares and understands

Unresolved Grief

Unresolved grief
Anger and pain
Buried inside
A muted refrain

Unresolved grief
A loss without hope
Unable to fathom
We try hard to cope

Pushing down under, with silence to spare
Covered in sadness and unspoken prayers

Unresolved grief
With silence to kill
It's a deadly destruction
Not cured with a pill

Unresolved grief
With tentacles long

Destroys all our passions
Our hope and our song

Pushing down under to not feel the pain
Creating for us a mournful refrain

Comfort for the Sorrowing

Comfort for the sorrowing
Comfort for the soul
Comfort for the grieving
Who are wanting to be whole

Comfort for the lonely
Comfort for the worn
Comfort for the weary
Whose lives are tattered, torn

Comfort for the fearful
Comfort for the lost
Comfort for the sinners
Whose lives are tempest tossed

Lord, grant to us your comfort
That only You can give
Grant to us your comfort
And show us how to live!

The Good Fight

He fought the good fight
He soared to the end
He was someone's dear father
Husband and friend

We don't understand it
We don't know the "why"
I guess in the end
That's why we all cry!

Broken Button

A broken button
A bit of lace
I still remember her smiling face

Her aging hands
Her quiet ways
How many projects filled her days

Now, some I'm finding still undone
For she's gone to meet God's Son

The Old Man

The old man looked across his bed
Breathed his last, as prayers were said

Some thought a simple life, he'd led
"He loved his wife," his children said

He made each of his children proud
He'd talked a lot, and laughed out loud

He praised his God and kept his word
Now he is living with his Lord

Limitations

As we go along each day
We often wonder why
Like why we hurt
And why we've changed
And why we sometimes cry

In times like these
We must seek the Lord
To know his Love and Care
And to recall His Faithfulness
And seek His Truth in prayer

We must reflect on brighter days
When He showed to us His Ways
And remember precious truths
That brought us happy days

We need to look into His Word
When we don't quite understand
For our thoughts are not His thoughts
For we are merely Man

Tea

Oh, come dear friend
And sit with me
We'll share some time
We'll sip some tea

No need for words
To comfort me
Just be my friend
And sip some tea

Cleaning Closets

Cleaning closets
Straightening up
It's my life's work
My bitter cup

But oh, the comfort
That can be known
When a friend helps
Us in our home

This Thanksgiving

On this Thanksgiving
As we all gather 'round
Some chairs will be empty
For some folks are out of town

We'll miss their cheerful natures
Their jokes and winning ways
With love and with laughter
We'll remember brighter days

This will be our first Thanksgiving
Without them by our side
And we will all be saddened
Just to think that they have died

We'll all go through the motions
And our hunger we may fill
But we'll long to have them with us
And we know we always will

This Thanksgiving will be different
And harder sure than most

But we'll remember they'll be dining
With a most Delightful Host

As other days will follow
And more holidays appear
We'll ask our Heavenly Father
To help us make it through each year

Your Birthday

Your birthday is coming
No candles or cake
Your birthday is coming
No photos to take
Your birthday is coming
As it does every year
Your birthday is coming

How I wish you were here!

Seeing Parents Aging

Seeing parents aging
As they walk with limping gait
We slow down our pacing
Not forcing them to wait

We ask them simple questions
Of what they want to do
Remembering other times
That they told us what to do

Now we hear them talking loudly
Though they not angry be
We wonder if we're aging too
And what our fate might be

We listen for their breathing
We see if their face is red
It seems not so long ago
That they tucked us into bed

Though many years have vanished
With secrets stored away
We treasure happy memories
To get us through this day

Until

Wanting still to have a voice
Wanting still to have some choice
The aging woman stood her ground
As she looked all around

Though her health was failing fast
She wanted still her voice to last
Until the end when life was gone
Until she sang her heavenly song

Bedside Vigil

Sitting by her bedside
Counting every breath
Praying for recovery
This is no time for death

Holding on to her hand
That's warm and soft and sweet
We long for pain to subside
As she seeks to find relief

Lying on her back
As she fights the pain
Wanting to get up
But still needing some restrain

Inner fears collide
Confusion takes its toll
We offer words of comfort
As we try to soothe, console

Calling out to God
We ask His way to find
Seeking good health
Wholeness, peace of mind

My Mother

My mother died Monday some time before seven
Escorted by angels and transported to heaven

While I was making my plans for the day
My dear Lord beckoned and called her away

My father, my father, with grief-stricken heart
Sorts through his papers, unsure where to start
Distracted by images of love's final blow
He wonders in secret just where he should go

My aunt in her nightgown has just heard the news
She cries out to heaven, just wanting a view

My brother at work is unpacking a bag
The phone rings. He's startled.
No time for jet lag.

When

When you were still upon this earth
You, the one who gave me birth
You took my hand
And called my name
And I was never quite the same

I owe you life
I owe you love
For all the blessings from above

Now you're with God
In Heaven, I know
That's still some place I want to go.

Because

Because you loved me, I can be strong
Because you loved me, I can fight wrong
Because you loved me, I can be whole

Because you loved me
My heart pays a toll

Repeat Conversations

Repeat conversations
Of days and years gone by

Repeat conversations
Sometimes I want to cry

Repeat conversations
When will they all end?

Repeat conversations
Here we go again!

A Poem for My Father

When my father's mind was sharper
He could weave a clever tale
Filled with intrigue and with passion
His imagination sailed

Now his body's growing weaker
And his mind is growing dim
Please remember my dear father
And the dreams he has within

My Father

My father has died and my mother is gone
Am I but an orphan trying to find home?
Am I but a daughter with burdens to bear?
Am I but a pilgrim in need of a prayer?

My father has died and my mother is gone
Help me dear Jesus to still carry on
Help me dear Jesus my burdens to bear
Help me dear Jesus to find you in prayer

Some Day

Some day when I am older
And see things that might have been

I'll remember days unending
When I listened once again
I'll have a new perspective
Not burdened down with care

Of my father gently smiling
As his laughter fills the air!

Who Knows?

Who knows sorrow?
Who knows pain?

Who knows suffering?
Who knows strain?

Who knows turmoil?
Who knows fear?

Oh, dear God,
I'm glad you're here!

Why?

Why does our ear long for a rhyme
A witty phrase, measured in time

Why does our face long for a smile
When life's been too tough for such a long while

Why does our heart long for a friend
When we feel hurt and in need of a mend

Why does our mind race back to the past
When moments flee and good times pass

Why does our soul long for a prayer
When God seems remote and we're filled with care

The whys and the wherefores may all come and go

But God is our Anchor
Of this truth, I know

The Road

I was walking down the Road of Life
Filled with good times, joy, some strife

When suddenly, without a look
A new Road appeared; one I took

The Road was rugged and filled with care
It brought sickness, death, despair

I learned it was the Road of Grief
The path of questions, of disbelief

I learned it was the Road of Tears
With untold doubts of pain and fears

The Road of Grief seemed far too long
I felt so empty; without a song

But as I walked down this Road of Gloom
I passed a cross, an empty tomb

I paused to listen. I paused to look.
And soon I found an ancient book.

I stopped to read. I stopped to pray.
I cried some tears along my way

As I continued down this path
I saw a Light. I saw a staff.

I felt a warmth. I felt a touch.
I knew somehow God loved me much

Soon I heard a quiet voice
I paused to listen, without choice

I stopped to ponder
I stopped to pray

Someone called me on that day
I heard a voice of Hope and Peace

I was restored
Such sweet release!

Poems and Prayers for the Grateful Heart

An Artist's Touch

An artist is an observer
Of the finest of things
Daffodils and sunsets
Babies and kings

An artist takes notice
Of things not yet seen
A butterfly's cocoon
As it spreads its wings

A girl in delight
With her first found beau
A boy in the mud
With a frog near his toe

The shadows that fall
On a crisp autumn day
The joy of a mare
As she plays in the hay

So many delights
May be seen by a few
The artist reminds us

We have a "room with a view"

If only we look
At Nature's sweet plans
And see God's Handiwork

Then...
We might understand

Faces

We see faces everyday
Some with smiles that make our day
Some with cares, with grief, and pain
While some have scars that still remain

Some are joyful, filled with love
Some angelic, as from above
Some are burdened down with care
While others seem, almost unaware

Some are angry, some are rude.
Some are toothless; and some are crude
Some seem empty, some seem blank
While others show that their heart has sank

Some are funny, laughing still
Their merry hearts just fit the bill
Some are confused, and in dismay
Trying to get through, yet another day

Some faces shine, all aglow
These are the people, we'd love to know

Some hold secrets, some hold doubt,
While some aren't sure what it's all about

Some faces are covered with soot or soil
Following a time of heavy toil
Some are covered like a mask
While others seem so downcast

Some seem pompous. Others proud
Some faces frightful in a crowd
Some seem nervous. Others weak
While some seem like they want to speak

Some are determined. Some are firm
Pressing on from lessons learned
Some seem kind, while others shy
Still others seem to just ask, "why?"

Lord, as we look upon each face
May we strive to see God's Grace

God's Pebbles

We all are God's Pebbles
Spread out everywhere
Some seem insignificant
Some, beyond compare

As folks we go through life
Under God's watchful hand
He fashions each pebble
Though we don't quite understand

Beneath each dusty surface
The pebble gleams and shines
With each challenging situation
The pebble is refined

Waves

Waves dance over the gentle seas
Waltzing winds, a current breeze
Waves turn bluish green to white
As winds pick up and soon take flight

Waves get bigger with mighty power
Against the shore, each passing hour
Waves can sometimes lull to sleep
A thoughtful man, with dreams to keep

In the Shadows

In the shadows by the river
Oh, In the shadows by the stream
Oh, in the shadows by the river
You can feel especially blessed

Oh, In the shadows
Yes, in the shadows
In the shadows, by the stream
In the shadows by the river
You can feel especially blessed

Looking round you at the river
Looking round you by the stream
In the shadows by the river
You can feel especially blessed

Oh, In the shadows, in the shadows
When you gaze out at the stream
In the shadows by the river
You can feel especially blessed
Yes, you can feel especially blessed

Rewind

Why can't I go back again?
Rewind my life and start again

I'd like to relive the happy days
Of feeling glad; of love, of praise

I'd love to see my children small
Before they'd grown and gotten tall

I'd love to spend a quiet day
To hear them laugh and watch them play

I'd love to witness another spring
When love was all, my everything

When flowers bloomed for you and me
When we were young and feeling free

To other days I would rewind
To see my parents in their prime

To see my brother and all our pranks
To say "I love you" and just give thanks

I would rewind to long lost friends
And renew our ties once again

I'd love to linger
I'd love to look
If my life could be a book!

Celebration

A celebration
Time of Life

When Man and Woman
Become Man and Wife

An age-old plan
But one still true

For God has Given
Me to you!

Little Baby

Little Baby
Oh, so small
Will we ever see you tall?

Little Baby
Oh, so sweet
You are our family's special treat

We see your fingers
Your little toes
We love your face
Your little nose

We see you sleeping
With such a smile
We'd love to hold you
Our dear sweet Child!

Mystery Love

Mystery love, Creator's dream
A child is born, a precious scream

A mother's touch, a father's care
A sister's joy; a brother's prayer

A dimpled face, a crinkled nose
How soft the skin; how sweet the toes!

How loud the cry! How bright the face!
How much the love! Such sweet embrace!

A Mother's Legacy

Through baby times and crazy times
And all the in-betweens
Through play dates and classmates,
A mother has her dreams

Through late nights and date nights
She learns how to forgive
Through her lifetime of loving
Her child learns how to live

A Father's Love

A father's love protects his little ones from fear
A father's love provides over many, many years

A father's love is deep and full of grace and pride
A father's love is strong, with lots of joy inside

A father's love is pure and only wants the best
A father's love gives hope so each will do their best

Repairs

Dads try to fix things
With nails and with glue
Moms try to fix things
Like broken hearts too

Dads try to fix things
Like houses and cars
Moms try to fix things
Like friendships and scars

When things are broken
And in need of repair
It is good to have a fixer
Who is very near

Every Time

Every time we turn around
We get the chance to prove
That Love is more
Than sweet romance
Or getting in the mood

Love is work and Love is hard
And Love can make us strong
It's about forgiveness when
Someone's done us wrong

Love can be about exhaustion
Or taking out the trash
Or letting someone
Choose his clothes
When we know they'll never match

Love lets another get in line
When we'd like to have first place
It's cheering for our child
Even though he's lost the race

Love is speaking up and shutting up

206

When we sometimes want our say
Love is listening to our family
When we'd rather have our way

Love is praying hard and playing long
And overcoming fears
It's laughing and packing
And making memories through the years

Love is fixing and frying
And giving kids a bath
Love is dreaming
And redeeming
And spending lots of cash

Love's a gift, a joy, a headache
A responsibility

Love makes us sweeter
Stronger, fuller than
We thought we'd ever be!

How Long's A Mother's Love?

How long's a mother's love?
Can it stretch around the moon

Can it wind its way to Africa
And be back again by noon

Can it soar o're the mountains
Or go underneath the sea

Through many different pathways
I've meant to set you free

I've meant to give you courage
So you alone could soar

Have I opened every window
And helped you find each door

Have I given you the guidance
Of a mother's love

Have I prayed enough in secret
To the Father up above

For I know that I'm not perfect
And my love's not always true

But I hope I've made a difference
In this big world for you

So now that you are leaving
And we soon will be apart

I offer you my prayers
But I give to you my heart!

A Parent's Prayer

Lord help us love our children well
As we teach them how to pray
May they learn the path of truth
As they learn how to obey

Teach us Lord how to be tough
And tender too with love
Give us wisdom when we pray
For strength from You above

Help us when we're overcome
With fear/anxiety
Help us Lord to know your truth
When Your Hand we do not see

Put a hedge of your protection
Around our hearts, Oh Lord
May we follow in your footsteps
And be of one accord

Lord, protect our children
From the Evil One

Help us to be devoted, Lord
To you Living, Loving Son

Thank you, Lord for giving us
The sweet gift of a child
Help us Lord to love them still
Though they be meek or wild

Family Reunion

Family reunion
What a wonderful thing
A time for catching fireflies
Or learning new songs to sing

A time for taking pictures
And watching babies grow
And sharing in the laughter
That families ought to know

Family reunion
We know it comes each year
Even though we're older
It still seems especially dear

It's a time for sharing memories
Of your mother and your dad
And playing with your cousins
Who always make you glad

Family reunion
We hope you'll come back soon

Bring some of your kinfolk
We're sure to find them room

It's a time to come together
When we've somehow grown apart
It's a time for making memories
And a blessing for the heart

Never the Same

Never the same
Never the same
When God intervenes
We are never the same

Never the same
Oh no, never the same
When God intervenes
We are never the same

The Bond of Mother/Daughter

Heartstrings born in heaven many years ago
A mother's love was forming
With so much love to show

A mother filled with wonder
With joy and love to share
Caring for her infant with hope beyond compare

As baby grows through childhood
With fun and play and smiles
Their tender love was growing

As daughter showed her style
Graced with love eternal
As mother led the way

Caring for her offspring
As she worked and played

Sometimes there were conflicts
Sometimes angry words
But always there was love between these special girls

As beauty turned to laughter
And wrinkles found their mark
A deeper love was growing

From an eternal spark
As boyfriends turned to husbands
And babies came to be

The bond of mother daughter was a joy for all to see

Through changes, fears and triumphs
The women's love still grew
Like a full-bloomed flower, as dreams they did pursue

As twilight turned to sunset
And flowers lost their bloom

Their love returned to heaven
Where God would find them room

Mystic Dreams

Exploring the harbor and colonial lore
Winding through towns on our way to the shore

Tasting the seafood, enjoying ice cream
It was all a part of our Connecticut dream

Sharing old times with laughter and tears
Reminiscing about the best of our years

Solving world problems, a swim in the lake
Eating the best pies made in the state

Seeing the shipyards, the colonial inns
We can hardly wait to do it again

The old Mystic Harbor with its proud ships
Were such delights of a wonderful trip

Viewing the covers of the Saturday Post
Selecting the ones that we liked the most

Norman Rockwell's vision of the American Dream
Honoring family, faith, and daily routines

Museums and shops and wineries too
Such were the adventures
That we shared with you

Quiet conversations and vigorous roars
Added so much to our trip to the shore

Looking at pictures of days all gone by
Wondering when we'd eaten more pie

Sharing great meals and times in your homes
We are so thankful as we fly our way home!

The Older Couple

The older couple on the beach
Holding hands, extending reach
Wrinkled tan from sun and age
Enjoying life, another stage

There was a day when love was new
And passions danced against the blue
When love grew strong
Like cresting waves
When hearts were full
With secrets saved

There was a day when dreams were cast
Creating memories born to last
The older couple by the sea
Living love eternally

Retirement Dreams

Every day we've gotten up
And done a job or two

Every day we've made a plan
Of what we had to do

Every day we've set aside
A wish, a dream, a care

Because we promised others
That we would just be there

But now the time is coming
When old dreams may reappear
And we need to start to listen
As we plan for future years

The dreams and hopes we've cherished
May still call from our soul
Though they may be hard to render
As we fear we're growing old

But let these inner voices
Speak kindly to our hearts
Suggesting new beginnings
As we plan a brand-new start

Grandson of Love

Grandson of love be born
On this special night
May God grant you life
As you come to us this night

Though our eyes have never seen you
And our hands have never touched
We have thought of you so often
And prayed for you so much

Grandson of love be born
On this special night
May God grant you entry
Into Earth's special light

Though your folks have never seen you
And your hands have never touched
They have prayed for you so often
And they love you very much

Your sisters have been sleeping
Tucked in their trundle beds

They may be having dreams of you
That turn often in their heads

Your uncles, aunts, and cousins
All hope to welcome you
We've all prepared a special place
In our hearts for you

So as you move in darkness
In a most mysterious place
We ask for God's great blessing
As He shows to us your face

Christmas Lullaby

Oh, little child, oh little babe
It's time that you learned
Of that First Christmas Day

Oh, little one
Hear of God's Son
Christ came to Earth
To give us new birth

Oh, little child, learn of God's way
How God showed his love
On that first Christmas Day

Stars shining bright
Bringing God's Light
Shepherds attend
God's love to send

Hear the bells ring
Birth of a King
God came to man
To show us His plan

Oh, little child, learn of God's way
How God showed his love
On that First Christmas Day

God sent his Son
To everyone
New life to bring
Our heavenly King

Angels proclaimed
God's Holy Name
Men from the East
Found God's Prince of Peace

Oh, little child, oh little babe
we're glad that you learned
Of that First Christmas Day

The New Year

Ringing in the New Year might be a lot of fun
But as we turn to face it, we might be feeling rather glum

Perhaps we feel that the old days were the best of all
Perhaps we fear that a new year might
not be that great at all

But God has established each new
year to implement His plan
That everyone throughout the world
would know God's love to man

To know a Savior who lived and died
that we might find true peace
To know our sins can be forgiven and we can find release.

So as we face a brand New Year; not
knowing what's in store
It's time to pray to Jesus and ask Him to show us more....

More of His Love, More of His Grace,
More of His Wonderous Power
More of His Provisions as He cares for us each hour

It's time to ask what we can do to
make this an awesome year
Do we need to trust God more and
share with Him our fears?

Do we need to offer thanks for blessings from above?
Do we need to honor Him and thank God for his love?

Do we need to ask the Lord to give us strength each day?
To help us be His instruments in every kind of way?

Do we need to hear His Word so we can finish strong?
Have we prayed to Jesus when someone's done us wrong?

Have we offered hope and care to others whom we know?
Have we asked for guidance so our love for God will grow?

Whatever we may face this year, we all must understand
That it is God who holds our future
and wants to hold our hand

To lead us into His Great Love and show us mercies true
So let's begin a brand New Year and see what God will do!

A Grandmother's Prayers

Stretching across many miles
And far above the seas

A grandmother's prayers
Reach the heart of God
As she prays on aching knees

In quiet whispers in the night
She shares her tales of love

With the Savior she has come to know
For the child she's come to love

She remembers oh so well
The day that each was born

The pure excitement and the joy
Of holding a newborn

She recalls counting toes
As she offered her sweet kiss

She remembers many nights
When a grandchild was dearly missed

She remembers special times
When her grands were not yet tall

When they would read a funny book
Or play with a bat and ball

Day and night her prayers go up
As she utters forth her pleas

Whether for a broken heart
Or for broken battered knees

She prays for her grown children
As they go along their way

That they will treasure each new child
And follow in God's ways
She thanks her Lord for special gifts
She's received along the way

Pictures, and homemade cards
With words her grands would say

As her prayers continue on
And her grands move on in life

She asks her Lord to bless each one
Keep them from fear and strife

She prays for safety for each child
Whether big or small

She prays that God will show them grace
And help them when they fall

She prays her grands will know her Lord
Whom she's loved for many years

And they will come to know God's truth
That will guide them through their tears

Golden Dreams

Waiting, anticipating
Putting patience to the test

Planning, changing
Making sure to do our best

Striving, reaching
For our highest goals

Dreams still teach us
Even though we've growing old

Helping Hands

In this world of many needs, we thank you, Lord
For the people who offer helping hands

Hands that comfort and hands that carry
Hands that direct and hands that deliver

Hands that bring and hands that brighten
Hands that gather and hands that give

Hands that mend and hands that multiply
Hands that pray and hands that provide

Hands that help and hands that heal
Hands that receive and hands that restore

Hands that serve and hands that save
Lord, thank you for all the helping hands

A Crooked Smile

You may wear a crooked smile
So what!
You may wear a crooked grin
So what!

It doesn't really matter to me
As long as you still smile

Our bodies may be changing
And our minds are re-arranging
But one thing that's never changing
Is my love for you

You may wear a crooked smile
So what!
You may wear a crooked grin
So what!

We've been through thick and thin
And I'd it all again
Because I love you

Our bodies may be changing
And lives are re-arranging

But one thing that's never changing
Is my love for you!

God's Presence

God is ever present
In our time of need

When we're feeling so afraid
And just can't seem to breathe

He is closer than a brother
Or our dearest human friend
He will never leave us, nor forsake us
And His Love will never end.

Spared

Looking up with fearful eyes
You were collapsed to my surprise
Your hands were clinched against the wheel
The van sped on. What an ordeal!

Our daughters cried yet calm prevailed
We prayed to God as our van sailed
On the highway at full speed
Without a break, without our lead

Yet faith took hold and Angels too
As our daughters tried to rally you
We spoke the truth; that God would aid
We prayed to God, we'd all be saved

And then somehow you came to
But our ordeal was not quite through

I steered the van with heaven's aid
While fighting fear, I hoped and prayed

Swerving through construction zones
I felt God's power and not my own

Coming to a welcomed spot
I wondered what would be our lot

But strangers stopped and hope prevailed
As I wondered if your heart had failed

Calls were made; medics to come
Emotions raged. Yet, I was numb

And yet, a quiet grace was given
For it was not your time for heaven!

Anchor of My Soul

He's the Anchor for my Soul
He's the Anchor for my Soul
Oh, Jesus is the Anchor for my Soul

Sometimes I get discouraged
And I start to drift away
But Jesus is the Anchor for my Soul

Make Him the Anchor of your Soul
The Anchor for Your Soul
Oh, oh, Jesus is the Anchor for my Soul

Sometimes, I get discouraged
And I start to slip away,
But Jesus is the Anchor for My Soul

The Seen and Unseen

Just below the surface
Of our tangled lives
Are many circumstances
Which may take us by surprise

Hidden repercussions
Of dreams and fears once known
Can be transformed by God
When we take them to His Throne

We may see God's Hand upon us
When we reflect upon our past
And rejoice with others
When God is using us at last!

Detours

Throughout life we chart our plans
To take a certain course
We set our goals, devise a plan
And move, without remorse

We plot our course, without a thought
Of what God may have in store
We move ahead and take some risks
While God might hope for more

While we try to make our way
God may have a different plan
We may be "stopped dead in our tracks"
And we don't quite understand

God in His grace may teach us things
That we have never known
He may reveal to us great truths
And take us to His Throne

God may put forth a brand-new quest
That we might never see

But we know, in His Great Love
That He sees Eternity

So, as we go through each new day
With many things to do
Let's remember to seek Him first
And He'll show us what to do!

Notecards and Postcards

Notecards and postcards
Letters and dreams
Pictures and paintings
And eating ice cream

Trophies and triumphs
And treasured delights
Such are the prizes
Of a wonderful life

Treasures

Clutter, clutter everywhere
Dust and lint upon my chair

Selling treasures, what a mess
It puts my mind in such distress

An antique lamp, a treasured book
So many things to fill each nook

A long-lost game; a doll, a toy
Buried treasure for girl or boy

So many years of gathered stuff
We must let go; enough is enough

Pass it on to someone else
It's been too long upon my shelf!

Moving Memories

Memories fade upon my chair
As I remember rocking there
Newborn babies, sweet and small
Smiling, eating, watch them crawl

Little ones with girly lace
Remembering each smiling face
Laughing, playing, watch them run
Many seasons filled with fun

School days, late nights start to fade
As my memories promenade
Moving memories stay with me
Lord bless our lives and families

Life

Though life isn't easy
It still can be grand
As we trust in Our Savior
And He takes our hand

Guiding our steps
Through life's weary days
Like a Tender Shepherd
He still guides our way

Though our path may be weary
He is faithful and strong
He carries us gently
When our days are too long

He comforts us sweetly
In the still of the night
For He is our Savior
And He's won the fight!

A Dream of Heaven

I walked along a beaten path
Not sure where it would go

The trees and meadows circled me
As a river ebbed and flowed

I felt the quiet gentle breeze
That marks the sign of spring

Around a bend, over a hill
I saw the home place of a King

Flowers bloomed and trees adorned
This peaceful holy place

And I was struck and quite amazed
That I'd reached this heavenly space

I saw friends and family there
And some I did not know

They waited for the King to pass
With faces all aglow

I longed to join in the fray
And add my voice of praise

I longed to be a part
Of this Celebration Day!

My Mother's Letter

I read my mother's letter
A few short hours ago
It felt like a heavenly visit
With the mother I loved so

She wrote of happy memories
Of families, friends and such
She wrote of special holidays
With those she loved so much

I read my mother's letters
She wrote of some who'd passed
On to a heavenly mansion
Where they'd see their Lord at last

She wrote of trusting Jesus
For faith and hope and love
She wrote of her desire to see
Loved ones up above

Though I miss my mother dearly
And would love to have her near

I know she's in a better place
Away from toil and fear

Though I long to see her
And would love to see her smile
I know she's with our Savior
And I'll join her after while

Time

Measured in moments
History and years
Filling our days with laughter and tears

Ticking so quietly
Day after day

We suddenly look up
Without words to say

Time is our healer
Our lover, our friend

Time will be with us
At least 'til the end

Time is our keeper
Our pulse and our life

It measures our worries
Our joy and our strife

It captures our interest

As special days pass
We remember with sadness
That Time may not last

Time marches on
As poets recite
It is more than a passing
It is our very life

CPSIA information can be obtained
at www.ICGtesting.com
Printed in the USA
BVHW041103120922
646801BV00014B/260/J

9 781669 844174